Fabiny, Sarah,

Who was Norman Rockwell? /

Who Was
Norman Rockwell?

by Sarah Fabiny

illustrated by Gregory Copeland

Penguin Workshop

To the Four Freedoms—SF

For Natalie, Gretta, and Lauren—GC

PENGUIN WORKSHOP
An Imprint of Penguin Random House LLC, New York

Text copyright © 2019 by Sarah Fabiny. Illustrations copyright © 2019 by Penguin Random House LLC. All rights reserved. Published by Penguin Workshop, an imprint of Penguin Random House LLC, New York. PENGUIN and PENGUIN WORKSHOP are trademarks of Penguin Books Ltd. WHO HQ & Design is a registered trademark of Penguin Random House LLC. Printed in the USA.

Visit us online at www.penguinrandomhouse.com.

Library of Congress Cataloging-in-Publication Data is available upon request.

ISBN 9780448488646 (paperback)   10 9 8 7 6 5 4 3 2 1
ISBN 9781524790967 (library binding)   10 9 8 7 6 5 4 3 2 1

Contents

Who Was Norman Rockwell?

In June 1993, almost fifteen years after Norman Rockwell died, the Norman Rockwell Museum opened in Stockbridge, Massachusetts. Stockbridge is the town where Norman had lived and worked for the last twenty-five years of his life. And this new museum had been built to hold the largest collection of Norman Rockwell art in the world.

The opening of the museum was a special occasion. Many people who had posed for Norman were there. His sons planted a tree in his memory. Children played and ran around the beautiful lawn and museum grounds. The crowd sang "America the Beautiful." The day was like a scene from one of Norman's own paintings! According to an article in the *New York Times*,

"The sun was shining brightly, of course. The sky was blue and the weather was temperate. There were Boy Scouts and Girl Scouts . . . antique fire engines and a four-clown band. It was an all-American Day. A Norman Rockwell day."

Norman Rockwell painted scenes that

captured the everyday experiences of Americans. His paintings made people feel special. They also made people think, laugh, and sometimes cry. They reflected the lives of ordinary Americans. And they often seemed to give people hope.

CHAPTER 1
A Boy with a Pencil

Norman Perceval Rockwell was born on February 3, 1894, in New York City. He was the second child of Nancy Hill Rockwell and Jarvis Waring Rockwell. Their firstborn son, Norman's brother, Jarvis, was a year and a half older than Norman.

When Norman was born, the Rockwells lived on the fifth floor of a brownstone building on the Upper West Side of Manhattan. At the time, the neighborhood was a bit rough and tough. There were a few street gangs who liked to start fights. Norman and his older brother did their best to stay out of trouble.

The kids in the Rockwells' neighborhood spent a lot of time playing games, like tag and touch football. Jarvis was athletic and good at sports.

Brownstones

In the 1890s, when Norman Rockwell was born, New York City had a population of just over 1.5 million people. Today more than 8.5 million people live there!

The city is made up of five boroughs: Manhattan, Brooklyn, the Bronx, Queens, and Staten Island. Some of the neighborhoods in these boroughs are famous for their brownstone buildings, which are usually just called "brownstones." They are given that name because of the dark stone that was used to cover the front of the buildings. It was less expensive than stone such as limestone, granite, and marble. Some brownstones were built for just one family. But many were apartment buildings for multiple families. They were affordable homes for the working class.

He got picked for teams all the time. But Norman was skinny and clumsy, and he hardly ever got chosen to be on a team. Fortunately, Norman was good at something else: He could draw.

The Rockwell home was a quiet, serious place. Some nights Norman's father would sketch copies of pictures from magazines. Norman would sit and watch him. He would try to copy what his father drew. Norman's father also read aloud to the family at night. As his father read, Norman would draw the characters in the story. He would imagine what they looked like and how they acted. Some of the books he read were by the famous British author Charles Dickens.

Charles Dickens (1812–1870)

Charles Dickens wrote some of the world's most famous books. He was born into a poor family and left school at the age of fifteen. Charles had several jobs after leaving school, and he  hated all of them. In 1836, he finally got a job that he liked: the editor of a literary magazine. While he was working there, he decided to start writing.

Many of Charles Dickens's books are about the hard life and times of working-class people in Victorian England. Dickens based some of them on his own life experiences. The characters in his books feel realistic because he came from a poor background himself. Some of his most famous books are: *Oliver Twist*, *A Tale of Two Cities*, *A Christmas Carol*, *David Copperfield*, and *Great Expectations*.

Norman's father was a textile salesman—he sold fabric. Norman's mother was a homemaker. Mrs. Rockwell was often sick, and she stayed in bed a lot. So Norman and Jarvis were often left to look after themselves. Norman's father fussed over his ill wife and took care of her. But he didn't pay much attention to his sons. Because of this, Norman did not always feel loved at home, and he sometimes felt very alone. Those feelings stayed with Norman throughout his life.

At least Norman had his drawing. He was able to find comfort and happiness while he was sketching. And he was good at it. Norman began to wonder if maybe this was something that he could do for a living.

Norman's eighth-grade teacher saw that he had talent. She encouraged him to draw pictures to go along with his reports. Norman loved doing this.

He drew Revolutionary War soldiers and covered wagons for his history reports, and bears, lions, and elephants for his science reports. Norman's teacher even allowed him to fill the chalkboards with drawings. The other students were impressed by Norman's work. And Norman was proud and excited that people appreciated it.

Every summer, the Rockwell family left New York City to spend time in the country. The family usually went to a farm in the Catskill Mountains in upstate New York. It was a big change for Norman and Jarvis. In the country, they swam in ponds, fished in lakes, went  on hayrides, and looked for frogs. Norman loved this time away from the city. He loved the

fresh air, green grass, and peace and quiet. Plus, he didn't have to worry about watching out for the neighborhood bullies. Later in his life, the memories of these summers played a big part in his career as an illustrator.

As he got older, Norman was determined to make his dream of becoming an artist come true. He decided that the best way to make this happen was to go to art school. Norman's parents didn't really support his choice, but they did not stop him. Norman got part-time jobs to help save money to pay for school. He delivered mail, mowed lawns, and even taught sketching to

a famous actress. With the money he made, Norman was able to sign up for classes at the New York School of Art, popularly known as the Chase School, in New York City. After some time there, he switched to the National Academy of Design.

In 1906, when Norman was twelve, the Rockwells moved out of New York City to a suburb called Mamaroneck. Twice a week Norman traveled by trolley, train, and subway to get to his classes in New York City. It took him

two hours each way. Norman often felt too tired to make the journey. But he was determined to become an artist, and that was what he needed to do. Besides, Norman loved his classes. He was with other students who were interested in the same things as he was. It didn't matter anymore that Norman was tall and skinny, with a big Adam's apple and spaghetti arms. All anyone cared about was how well he could draw.

However, Norman soon realized that he would not be able to keep up with this schedule. It was too hard to go to high school in Mamaroneck, work part time, and take art classes in New York City. So at the end of his junior year, Norman dropped out of high school. He decided to enroll full time at an art school called the Art Students League. It was one of the most famous art schools in the country. So, at the age of seventeen, Norman packed his bags and pencils and headed back to New York City.

The Art Students League, New York City

CHAPTER 2
A Serious Student

Norman started classes at the Art Students League in October 1911. For the next three years, Norman learned as much as he could about drawing and illustrating. Every day, Norman and the other male students packed into rooms with their pads of paper and charcoal, ready to draw.

(There were female students at the Art Students League, but men and women were not allowed to be in the same classes.) Norman and his fellow students sketched models and studied the human form. One of their teachers, George Bridgman, used a skeleton to show how complex the body was and how all its parts worked together.

George Bridgman teaching his art students

The Art Students League had been started by a group of art students, including Howard Pyle. He

Howard Pyle

was one of the most famous illustrators of the "Golden Age of Illustration" at the end of the 1800s. Norman thought Howard Pyle was one of the greatest illustrators *ever*. Other famous illustrators working during that time were Winslow Homer, Frederic Remington, and N. C. Wyeth. Illustrators are artists whose work appears in books, magazines, and sometimes calendars and greeting cards, instead of in museums or art galleries. They draw with pencils and pastels and paint as well. Norman admired the work these illustrators did. He liked how they made characters come to life and made you feel as if you were in the picture.

Norman felt that being an illustrator was "a profession with a great tradition, a profession I could be proud of."

Text illustration created by Frederic Remington

Norman took his classes at the Art Students League very seriously. So seriously that his classmates called him "the Deacon." The other students would go out to enjoy the sights, sounds, and nightlife of New York City. Many worked whenever they felt like it, sometimes in the middle of the night. But Norman would never miss lunch, and he never worked through the night. He had very strict habits, and he didn't let anything distract him from them.

Another teacher at the Art Students League was Thomas Fogarty. Norman loved the assignments he gave the students. Mr. Fogarty would select a story from a magazine and ask the students to read it. He then told the students

Thomas Fogarty

to choose a scene from the story to illustrate. Mr. Fogarty challenged the students to "live in the picture." He wanted them to feel like they were living with the characters they drew.

At the end of his first year at the Art Students League, Norman won a scholarship in Thomas Fogarty's class. And one of his drawings was judged the best illustration of the year. The illustration, called *The Deserted Village*, is based on a poem by Oliver Goldsmith. The drawing shows a young boy who is sick, lying in bed. A preacher is kneeling alongside. A grandfather clock looms in the background, and a single candle lights the room. It is a very dramatic scene, and it tells a story. We get the feeling that the sick boy may not get better.

The Deserted Village illustration

Thomas Fogarty recognized that Norman had real talent. He was sure that Norman would be able to make a living as an illustrator. He convinced Norman to show his portfolio (samples of his work) to a publishing company. The publishing company was impressed with what Norman showed them. They asked him to create some illustrations for a children's book called *Tell Me Why: Stories about Mother Nature*. Norman was paid $150 to create twelve paintings. He was only eighteen years old, but Norman was on his way to becoming a real illustrator.

One of Norman Rockwell's illustrations from *Tell Me Why*

With the money Norman had made from the book illustrations, he was able to rent a studio. He was also able to tell book and magazine publishers that he was already a published illustrator. Norman went to visit the offices of the Boy Scouts of America. The Boy Scouts published a magazine called *Boys' Life* and now wanted to create a handbook for Boy Scouts. They asked Norman to create some illustrations for the handbook. The editor of the handbook was so pleased with what Norman drew that he asked Norman to become the art editor of *Boys' Life*. It was up to Norman to decide which illustrations would go in the magazine every month. He was only nineteen at the time. His salary was fifty dollars a month.

Besides being the art editor, every month Norman also illustrated one story and painted the cover for the magazine. The Boy Scouts also published a calendar every year. Over the next sixty years, Norman would create many covers

for the Boy Scout calendar.

But this wasn't the only work that Norman did. He also illustrated advertisements for cereal, toothpaste, cough medicine, and socks. His name was becoming well-known, and people were beginning to recognize his drawings. More and more companies wanted him to work for them.

Steven Spielberg, Boy Scout

When he was a young boy, Steven Spielberg—
one of the world's most famous movie directors—
saw a poster at a Boy Scout meeting in Scottsdale,
Arizona. The poster was titled *The Spirit of America*.
It featured a Boy Scout, a pilot, a soldier, and a

Native American, with presidents Washington, Lincoln, and Theodore Roosevelt in the background. Spielberg remembers that it "gave us an image to aspire toward."

When Spielberg became a movie director, he took inspiration from "The Spirit of America" and all of Norman's covers for the Boy Scout calendars. He wanted to achieve in his movies what Norman had captured in his art: true emotion and feeling. And with movies like *E.T. the Extra-Terrestrial*, *Raiders of the Lost Ark*, *Jurassic Park*, *The BFG*, and *Ready Player One*, he obviously has.

For an illustrator, the "greatest show window in America," Norman once said, was illustrating a cover for *The Saturday Evening Post*. One of Norman's biggest goals was to paint a cover for this magazine. Norman felt that if he could get his art on the cover of the *Post*, he would have proven himself as an illustrator. But Norman was nervous about asking the magazine for work. He

wasn't sure his work was good enough for *The Saturday Evening Post*. One of Norman's friends finally persuaded him to go to their offices in Philadelphia and show them some of his work.

Norman took two paintings and several sketches to show the magazine's editor, George Horace Lorimer. He waited patiently while Mr. Lorimer and the magazine's art editor studied his work. Norman couldn't believe it when they said that they loved it! They wanted to buy the two paintings and an additional sketch idea. And they also wanted Norman to do three new covers for the magazine.

George Horace Lorimer

The *Post* would pay him seventy-five dollars for each cover. "Wow!" Norman said later. "A cover on the *Post* . . . I had arrived."

The Saturday Evening Post

The Saturday Evening Post was considered "America's magazine." Its pages were filled with stories, news reports, cartoons, and illustrations. Millions of people subscribed to the weekly magazine and couldn't wait for it to show up on their doorsteps. Because there was no TV, radio, or Internet in the early 1900s, the magazine was how many Americans found out about what was happening in their country and around the world.

Great writers such as Edgar Allan Poe, F. Scott Fitzgerald, and Agatha Christie had stories published in the *Post*. And famous illustrators such as J. C. Leyendecker (one of Norman Rockwell's heroes), John Philip Falter, and N. C. Wyeth created covers for the magazine. But the most popular illustrator who worked for *The Saturday Evening Post* was Norman Rockwell.

Irene O'Connor

Norman was excited to tell his family about his good news. He was also excited to tell his girlfriend at the time, Irene O'Connor. In fact, he was so excited that he asked Irene to marry him. Norman was on his way to being a real illustrator, and his life was moving forward. Nothing could stop him now.

CHAPTER 3
On the Cover of a Magazine

Norman's first cover for *The Saturday Evening Post* appeared on May 20, 1916. He was only twenty-two years old at the time. The cover was called *Boy with Baby Carriage*, and it told a story that everyone could understand. It shows a boy, who is wearing his best clothes, pushing a baby carriage. His friends pass him as they head to play baseball. It is obvious that the boy pushing the carriage is unhappy that he has to babysit his little sister. And the two boys on their way to the game

are making fun of their friend. The message in the picture is very clear. The cover was a hit.

Norman continued to paint covers for *The Saturday Evening Post* that showed everyday people doing very common things. The covers showed everything from a young boy surprised when he finds a Santa suit in his parents' dresser, to an overweight chef reading a diet book, to a girl with a black eye smiling as she waits outside the principal's office. The illustrations were of ordinary people doing ordinary things. There were families, couples in love, animals, and lots of children.

Readers of the magazine loved how Norman painted situations and scenes that they could relate to. They saw themselves and their lives in his work. Norman was able to capture so much in a single illustration, whether it was funny, sad, or serious. He was able to tell a story without words. As one writer said about Norman's work, "He made the average American special."

Over the next forty-seven years, Norman would create more than 320 covers for *The Saturday Evening Post*. He also painted 158 story illustrations that appeared inside the magazine. Norman's covers for *The Saturday Evening Post* were so popular that when one appeared on the magazine, the *Post* printed an extra quarter of a million copies. They knew how much Americans loved Norman's images and how well they sold.

Norman always used real people as his models. The children in his pictures are based on the actual neighborhood kids who posed for him near his home in a suburb of New York City. Norman would pay them fifty cents an hour.

Norman wanted his pictures to be perfect. All the details had to be just right. So the children often had to pose for hours. It was hard work. It was tough to sit still for that long! To keep his young subjects focused, Norman would place a stack of nickels on a table to show them how much they had earned so far. Seeing the money they had made kept them from fidgeting.

Just as Norman's career with *The Saturday Evening Post* was getting firmly established, the United States declared war against Germany. It was April 1917, and Norman wanted to help in the war effort. He was determined to join the Navy. However, the recruiting office told Norman that he was too skinny to enlist.

He would have to gain weight before he could be accepted. So Norman stuffed himself with doughnuts, bananas, and water until he had gained the weight he needed.

The Navy sent Norman to Charleston, South Carolina. When they discovered he was a talented artist, they had Norman create portraits of many officers, their wives, and lots of sailors. And he

also drew cartoons for *Afloat and Ashore*, the Navy newspaper. Norman was also able to do other work while in the Navy. He was allowed to create covers for *The Saturday Evening Post*, as long as they had a military theme.

Norman was discharged from the Navy in November 1918. He returned to New Rochelle, New York, where he and Irene lived. He continued to paint covers for the *Post* and created advertisements for many products, including Fisk bicycle tires, Black Jack Gum, and Jell-O.

Jell-O ad illustration

People across the country and the world could now recognize an illustration by Norman Rockwell. He was becoming more and more famous, and he was working harder than ever. Norman painted every day, even on Christmas. He spent a lot of time getting his illustrations just right. He wanted them to be perfect, and he wanted everyone to love them.

Norman would spend hours and hours in his studio. But his wife, Irene, liked going out. When she and Norman were first married, they would go boating, play bridge, and golf with friends. They attended parties and invited people over to their house. However, as Norman spent more

time in the studio, their social life quieted down. Irene still wanted to go out, but Norman was happy to stay at home and work. Norman realized that he and Irene wanted different things from life. They divorced in 1929.

After the divorce, Norman decided to move back to New York City. He continued to work hard and create illustrations for *The Saturday Evening Post*. Everyone loved Norman's covers, but Norman didn't feel loved. He was on his own and lonely. Some friends invited him to visit them in California. They thought the warm temperatures, sunshine, and change of scenery might be good for him. Plus, his friends wanted him to meet a girl they thought would be perfect for Norman. Her name was Mary Barstow.

Mary Barstow

CHAPTER 4
A New Chapter

Mary Barstow was born in Illinois, but her family moved to southern California when she was in grade school. She was confident and bright. Mary graduated from Stanford University in 1929. After college, she became a schoolteacher, but Mary really wanted to be a writer.

Norman met Mary at a dinner party at the home of a friend. She was twenty-two, and he was thirty-six. Norman's friends were right: Mary was the type of woman he needed in his life. Norman asked Mary to marry him just two weeks after meeting her. They were married on April 17, 1930.

The couple moved to New Rochelle, New York, and Norman got back to work. Mary understood

how important her husband's career was to him.
She liked that Norman was serious about what
he did and wanted to be the best illustrator he
could be. Mary decided to help her husband with
his work. She often read to Norman while he
painted. She also took care of the bills, contracts,

and the rest of the paperwork. And Mary found props that Norman could use in his illustrations. Norman sometimes worried about whether his paintings were good enough. But Mary's support always helped him get through it.

Tom, Jarvis, Peter

The couple had three sons: Jarvis, born in 1931; Tom, born in 1933; and Peter, born in 1936. The three young boys kept Mary busy while Norman worked in his studio, but Mary continued to help Norman as much as she could.

Although Norman's paintings were very much in demand, he was feeling more insecure about his work. Norman felt it was time for a change.

After a trip to Europe, the Rockwell family moved to Arlington, Vermont, in 1938. The small New England town was a change from busy New Rochelle. It was peaceful, quiet, and friendly. Arlington reminded Norman of the places where he and his family had spent their summer vacations when he was a boy. The move was just what Norman needed.

Norman decided to turn a barn in Arlington into his studio. Lots of people in town dropped by the studio to watch their famous neighbor work. Many ended up modeling for Norman. Norman's neighbors also would bring him things he could use as props in his paintings. And Norman made time to take breaks from his work. He and Mary went square dancing every week. Norman felt happy again about his life and his work.

One night in the summer of 1942, Norman jumped out of bed with what he said was "the best idea I ever had." At that time, the United States had been involved in World War II for several months. Norman wanted to help somehow with the war effort. He had enlisted during World War I, but now he was too old to join the military. Norman's idea was to bring one of President Franklin D. Roosevelt's speeches to life.

The president had spoken about four freedoms that every citizen should have once the war ended: freedom of speech, freedom of every citizen to worship God in their own way, freedom from want, and freedom from fear. Norman was determined to paint each of these ideas in a way that Americans could understand.

Norman jumped on his bicycle and raced to his studio. He started sketching right away. He decided to use the people of Arlington as his models. He would draw the four freedoms as scenes from everyday life. A man speaking at a local town meeting portrayed freedom of speech.

The "Four Freedoms" Speech

President Franklin D. Roosevelt gave the "Four Freedoms" speech on January 6, 1941. At this point, the United States was not yet involved in World War II, and many people did not want the country to go to war. They felt that US involvement in World War I had been wrong, and Americans did not need to fight in another war. But President Roosevelt wanted people to understand that the United States had a responsibility to help its allies fight for democracy and for what is right. Every citizen around the world was entitled to the "four freedoms."

On December 7, 1941, eleven months after Roosevelt gave his speech, the Japanese bombed Pearl Harbor. Because of this, the United States decided to enter World War II. Americans knew that involvement in the war would be difficult for their country. Young men would be sent into battle. Many things would be rationed. But they also knew that the United States had to help fight for the four freedoms that Roosevelt had spoken about.

A family gathered for Thanksgiving dinner was Norman's idea of freedom from want. People of different faiths praying were his image for freedom of worship. And a couple tucking their children into bed showed freedom from fear.

Norman was excited about these four drawings. He felt that showing President Roosevelt's ideas as scenes from daily life would help Americans understand the importance of the four freedoms. Norman took the sketches to Washington, DC, to show them to some government agencies. But the agencies were not interested in Norman's sketches.

They said that for the war effort, they wanted work from "real artists" and not illustrators. Norman's excitement turned to disappointment. He was sad that the agencies didn't want his work and didn't see him as a real artist.

On his way back to Vermont, Norman stopped at the office of *The Saturday Evening Post* in Philadelphia. Norman showed his sketches of the four freedoms to a new editor there who liked the sketches very much. He wanted Norman to turn them into covers for the magazine. Norman promised to finish them in just a few months.

However, the paintings took Norman longer than he thought they would. It was difficult work. The paintings were very important to Norman, and he wanted them to be perfect. He struggled with every detail. Finally, six months later, the four paintings were finished.

The *Four Freedoms* ran as covers on *The Saturday Evening Post* in 1943. They were a huge success. The US Treasury Department decided to send Norman's actual paintings on a nationwide tour. Over one million people saw the paintings as they made their way across the country. Norman received letters from over seventy thousand people saying how much they loved the paintings!

Four Freedoms paintings

Because they were so popular, over $132 million worth of government war bonds were sold. The bonds raised money for the war effort. The agency that had originally said they wanted only "real artists" to work on posters for the war sold more than four million copies of the *Four Freedoms*.

These special paintings touched the hearts and minds of Americans. Norman hadn't had to join the military to help the United States fight the war. He was very proud. But this great moment was followed by tragedy. Just a few days after Norman sent off the *Four Freedoms* to *The Saturday Evening Post*, his studio burned down.

CHAPTER 5
The Move to Massachusetts

By the time the volunteer firemen reached Norman's studio, they were unable to save anything. All the paintings, sketches, brushes, paints, props, and costumes were gone. Norman even lost his Howard Pyle prints. "Well, there goes my life's work," said Norman. He was forty-nine years old. He had overcome difficult situations in his life, and now he would do it again. He made a sketch of the event called *My Studio Burns* for the *Post*. Then Norman built a new studio and got right back to work.

Norman's paintings changed after the fire. Although he had new brushes, easels, and paints, he had lost all the old-fashioned costumes and props he had collected. Over the years, he had

used them to illustrate scenes from the past. After
the fire, Norman no longer painted scenes with
early presidents, pirates, or pioneers. His work
focused more on the present.

The present situation that Norman focused on most was World War II. But he didn't paint scenes of soldiers fighting. Americans had loved his *Four Freedoms* that showed ordinary people. So Norman decided to paint Americans who were helping the war effort at home. Norman painted women factory workers making supplies for the soldiers, men listening to war reports on the radio, a returned soldier peeling potatoes for his mother, and many other everyday scenes.

One of the most famous paintings he did during this time was called *Rosie the Riveter*.

Rosie the Riveter

The painting shows a strong-looking woman with a rivet gun in her lap and a sandwich in her hand, taking her lunch break. It appeared on the cover of *The Saturday Evening Post* on May 29, 1943.

And when it looked like World War II was coming to an end, Norman painted scenes of soldiers returning to their families. The paintings helped Americans feel proud about the sacrifices they had made during the war.

In the late 1940s and early 1950s, Norman's work was more popular than ever. His name was known not only by Americans but by people all over the world. But Norman felt he needed another change. Once again he thought a new town and a new studio might inspire new ideas. Mary had not been well. And Norman hoped that moving closer to Mary's doctors would be better for the family. So in 1953, Norman and Mary moved to Stockbridge, Massachusetts.

The Wartime Workforce

During World War II, factories around the country were busy making tanks, vehicles, ships, airplanes, and weapons to be used in the war.

Many men who worked in those factories left their jobs to join the armed forces. Those jobs needed to be filled, so many factory owners hired women to keep their factories running. To inspire

women to take factory jobs, the US government came up with an advertising idea that featured a character called "Rosie the Riveter." Rosie was the symbol of strong, patriotic women who were proud to help their country during the war by taking jobs in factories and shipyards.

Just as they had immediately fit into Arlington, Vermont, Norman and Mary fit into Stockbridge right away. They became friends with the townspeople. Many wanted to model for Norman, and he soon found his favorites.

Models pose for Rockwell's painting *The Optician*

Not long after the Rockwells moved to Stockbridge, Norman painted *Breaking Home Ties*. The painting tells the story of a young man moving away from home. It was Norman's way of revealing what was happening in his own life. Jarvis had enlisted in the Air Force, and Tom and Peter were growing up and thinking about their futures. The painting reflects Norman's feelings about his sons leaving home. In the scene, a father and son are sitting next to each other on their truck. The son is heading to college. He is smiling nervously as he waits for the train that will take him there. The father isn't looking at the train or his son. He looks tired and sad that his son is off to start a new life.

The Rockwells enjoyed their life in Stockbridge. Mary looked after everything in their daily lives so that Norman could concentrate on his work. During this time, Norman painted some of his most memorable covers for *The Saturday Evening*

Post, including *Art Critic, Girl at the Mirror, Soda Jerk,* and *The Runaway.* These were all paintings showing one single moment in the subject's life. These weren't fancy or heroic people, just plain people being themselves.

Soda Jerk

In 1959, Mary died in her sleep of a heart attack. The couple had been married for twenty-nine years. The boys had all grown up and moved away, and Norman was alone in the Stockbridge house. Many of Norman's friends encouraged him to get out and do things. They didn't want him staying by himself and being sad.

Norman took his friends' advice and signed up for a poetry class. The class was taught by a retired teacher named Molly Punderson. She was surprised to have someone so famous in her class. She was also surprised at how humble Norman was. And Norman was impressed by how Molly could recite hundreds of poems by heart. Norman was glad he had listened to his friends' advice. The couple fell in love and were married on October 25, 1961. Later Norman said, "I don't know how I would have made it if it hadn't been for Molly."

Triple Self-Portrait

After his wife Mary's death, Norman Rockwell started one of his most famous paintings and one of the most famous paintings in American art: *Triple Self-Portrait.*

The painting shows Norman sitting in front of a canvas, looking at himself in a mirror as he paints. There are four pictures tacked to the right side of the canvas. They are self-portraits of the artists Albrecht Durer, Rembrandt van Rijn, Pablo Picasso, and Vincent van Gogh. These artists are all well-known for painting themselves. Rembrandt painted more than ninety self-portraits!

In this work, Norman is poking fun at the self-portrait as a form of painting. The viewer can see how Norman has made himself look better on the canvas than he looks in the mirror. He is humorously comparing himself to the master painters who are looking at him from their own self-portraits. *Triple Self-Portrait* appeared on the cover of the February 13, 1960, issue of *The Saturday Evening Post*.

Norman was happy with his home life. But *The Saturday Evening Post* was becoming less popular and fewer people were reading it. By the early 1960s, there were many other magazines for readers to buy. Most people now had televisions and got their news and entertainment from TV programming. The editors at the *Post* hoped that asking Norman to paint new and different kinds of covers would increase the magazine's popularity again.

The *Post* sent Norman around the world to paint portraits of world leaders. He sketched Jawaharlal Nehru of India, Gamal Abdel Nasser of Egypt, and Josip Broz Tito of Yugoslavia. At home, he painted portraits of American politicians such as Dwight Eisenhower, Richard Nixon, and John F. Kennedy. As always, Norman took great time and attention with these portraits. These were important men. He wanted to capture the details and their personalities perfectly.

Rockwell with his painting of Jawaharlal Nehru

Although the portraits were just what the *Post* wanted, they were not what Norman wanted. He missed creating pictures that told stories. He had a special talent for capturing life in a single moment, and he wanted to keep doing that. Norman felt that the *Post* no longer truly valued his talent. So in 1963, at the age of sixty-nine and after 323 covers, Norman stopped working for *The Saturday Evening Post*.

CHAPTER 6
Causes on Canvas

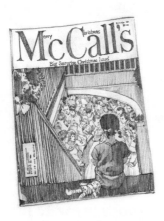

Norman could have retired. But when other magazines, such as *Look* and *McCall's* offered him work, Norman accepted. He called this his "late period." Norman saw this as an opportunity to go back to doing what he loved: telling stories with his illustrations. He was nearly seventy, and he was interested in capturing what was happening around him. Norman wanted to focus on issues that Americans were concerned about. Social problems—the issues that affect real life—had always been important to Norman. Now he had a chance to bring those subjects to life in his work. He said, "Now I am wildly excited about painting contemporary subjects . . . pictures about civil rights, astronauts, the Peace Corps, the poverty program. It's wonderful."

Look magazine told Norman to paint what he saw. They wanted their readers to see the world through the eyes of Norman Rockwell. One of the first paintings he did for *Look* was called *The Problem We All Live With*. The painting is based on a real event. It shows Ruby Bridges, a young African American girl, walking to an all-white school. She is escorted by four federal marshals— government police officers. Norman's painting captures every detail of the event, from Ruby's notebook, ruler, and pencils, to the smashed tomato and racial slur on the wall.

At the time, a new law had been enacted. It
said that African American children and white
children should go to the same schools. Up to this
time, black people and white people had always
been segregated, or kept apart. They couldn't go
to the same schools, sit together on buses, or drink
from the same water fountains. Many people in

the United States, especially in the South, had a hard time accepting this new law. Norman's painting and its title reflected the problem of racism that was happening in the country.

In 1967, Norman painted *New Kids in the Neighborhood*. It shows an African American family moving into a white neighborhood. The children, and the cat and the dog, are curiously studying one another. Even though they are unsure now, the painting also makes us feel hopeful that the kids will work it out. Soon they will be friends and playing together.

New Kids in the Neighborhood

The Civil Rights Act of 1964

On June 11, 1963, President John F. Kennedy gave a speech calling for a law that would give "all Americans the right to be served in facilities that are open to the public." He also said the law should "offer greater protection for the right to vote." President Kennedy began to work with Congress to pass this new civil rights bill. When President Kennedy was assassinated on November 22, 1963, Vice President Lyndon B. Johnson became president. He made this civil rights bill one of his top priorities.

President Johnson spent many hours with members of Congress and civil rights leaders, such as Martin Luther King Jr., to make sure the law would protect the rights of people who had been discriminated against.

On July 2, 1964, President Johnson signed the bill into law. Martin Luther King Jr. was standing at his side. The new law had eleven sections. These are some of the most important:

Title I—Anyone can register to vote and voting requirements must be the same for all people.

Title II—Discrimination in all public places, such as motels, restaurants, and theaters, is outlawed.

Title IV—Public schools can no longer be segregated.

Title VII—Discrimination by employers based on race, gender, religion, or national origin is outlawed.

During the 1960s and 1970s, Norman continued to paint what he saw. He wanted to tell the stories he felt needed to be told, whether they were happy, such as the Apollo 11 moon landing, or sad, such as the Mississippi murders of three civil rights workers. Norman had always painted America at its best, but now he was showing America exactly as it was. It was a difficult time for many Americans, but Norman's work, like the painting called *Southern Justice*, helped people understand the issues their country faced.

Southern Justice

Stockbridge, Massachusetts, was very proud of its most famous citizen. The town decided to honor him by declaring May 23 Norman Rockwell Day. And on May 23, 1976, the town held a parade for him. Norman was eighty-two years old at the time. He and Molly sat on a flatbed truck and watched the parade march down Main Street. Jarvis and Tom were there with their families.

Norman continued to go to his studio every day, but he didn't always paint. Going to the studio had become a habit. He liked spending time around the paint, brushes, and canvases. Sometimes he needed a wheelchair to get there, but Norman was happiest when he was in his studio.

CHAPTER 7
An Aging Artist

The United States of America celebrated its two hundredth birthday on July 4, 1976. There were celebrations across the country to mark this special anniversary. Norman decided to mark the occasion with a painting of himself wrapping a ribbon around the Liberty Bell. The painting, entitled *Liberty Bell (Celebration)* appeared on the cover of *American Artist* magazine. It was the last magazine cover that Norman painted.

Although it wasn't as detailed as Norman's earlier work, the painting still tells a story. The ribbon says "Happy Birthday," and Norman is carefully wrapping it around the bell. He is expressing how much he has enjoyed painting this great nation throughout his career. The cracked bell is a sign that America has flaws as well. But Norman is happy to embrace all that. He thought that America's flaws as well as its greatness are what make it so special.

The Liberty Bell in Philadelphia

Throughout his career, Norman had received thousands of letters from people who admired his work. He also received lots of honors and awards. Perhaps the greatest award Norman received came in a letter from President Gerald Ford. He had decided to present Norman with the Presidential Medal of Freedom. The medal is the nation's highest honor given to a civilian.

Gerald Ford

Norman was awarded the medal for his "vivid and affectionate portraits of our country and ourselves." Unfortunately, at this point, Norman was too frail to travel to Washington, DC, to accept his medal. Jarvis made the trip to accept the medal on behalf of his father.

The Presidential Medal of Freedom

The Presidential Medal of Freedom is an award presented by the president of the United States. The honor is given to people who have made "an especially meritorious contribution to the security or national interests of the United States, world peace, cultural or other significant public or private endeavors." The president decides who will receive each medal.

The Medal of Freedom was established by President Kennedy in 1963. Here are just a few of the people who have received the Presidential Medal of Freedom:

Sam Walton

- Walt Disney, 1964: movie producer and creator of Disneyland
- Georgia O'Keeffe, 1977: artist
- Sam Walton, 1992: founder of Walmart
- Sandra Day O'Connor, 2009: Supreme Court Justice
- Maya Angelou, 2011: writer and poet
- Steven Spielberg, 2015: movie director
- Bruce Springsteen, 2016: musician known as "The Boss"

Maya Angelou

By 1978, Norman was constantly cared for by nurses. But he still insisted on going to the studio every day. Norman had once said, "When I die, I want to be working on a picture and just fall over." Norman Rockwell died on November 8, 1978. There was an unfinished painting on the easel in his studio.

After Norman's death, the flags in Stockbridge were flown at half-mast as a sign of respect.

Hundreds of people attended his funeral. Cub Scouts and Boy Scouts stood along the entrance of the church to honor the artist who had painted their calendars for over fifty years. One of Norman's friends read a poem at the funeral service that Norman had always liked. The poem is about an angel writing in a golden book, who

visits a man during the night. The man asks the angel to note in his book that he is "one that loves his fellow men"—that he is someone who deeply cares about those around him. Norman saw himself as that person. He loved ordinary people, and he had devoted most of his career to painting them.

CHAPTER 8
An American Mirror

Many Americans were very sad when they heard the news that Norman Rockwell had died. Some art critics thought his work was too corny, or sentimental, or ordinary. But to many people, he painted "what was real for Americans, or at least what Americans wanted and hoped and prayed *could* be real."

Norman painted all of America, from quiet moments in everyday life to important moments in history. He painted two people eating at a restaurant and two men fighting in a boxing ring. He painted scenes from colonial America and one of astronauts landing on the moon. He painted scruffy kids with black eyes and serious

presidents. He painted peaceful country scenes and the country's most difficult struggles with civil rights.

In June 1993, the Norman Rockwell Museum moved to a new, larger location. Norman's red barn studio was moved to the grounds of the museum.

People came to see the brushes, paints, and easel he used, as well as his favorite chair. Thousands of people from around the world continue to visit the museum every year to see the studio and the hundreds of paintings and drawings on display.

Norman's paintings told stories. And Americans could see themselves, the people they loved, and their own lives in those stories. As President Ford said, "Norman Rockwell's art always indelibly reflected America as it was at its best."

When he died, Norman was seen as an illustrator and not a true artist. He wasn't considered to be as important as other artists, such as Jackson Pollock, Andy Warhol, Pablo Picasso, and Henri Matisse, who had worked during Norman's lifetime. But today he is recognized as a major artist.

His paintings have sold for millions of dollars: *Breaking Home Ties* sold for $15.4 million in 2006 and *Saying Grace* sold for $46 million in 2013. And Norman Rockwell's work is collected by two of the world's most famous movie directors: George Lucas and Steven Spielberg. Together they own more than fifty works by the artist.

The stories Norman Rockwell's paintings tell are timeless and universal—they are just as

Steven Spielberg and George Lucas exhibit Rockwell works from their collections

appealing today as when he first painted them. Norman Rockwell created paintings that became a mirror for the viewers' own emotions and memories.

They are now considered to be American masterpieces.

Where to Find Norman Rockwell's Paintings

- The Brooklyn Museum, Brooklyn, New York

- Corcoran Gallery of Art, Washington, DC

- The Metropolitan Museum of Art, New York, New York

- National Air and Space Museum, Washington, DC
- National Cowboy Museum, Oklahoma City, Oklahoma
- National Portrait Gallery, Washington, DC
- The Norman Rockwell Museum, Stockbridge, Massachusetts

Timeline of Norman Rockwell's Life

1894	February 3, born in New York City
1911	Enrolls at the Art Students League
1916	First cover illustration for *The Saturday Evening Post*
	Marries Irene O'Connor
1921	Paints *No Swimming*, one of his most famous paintings
1929	Divorces Irene O'Connor
1930	Marries Mary Barstow
1939	Moves to Arlington, Vermont
1943	*The Saturday Evening Post* publishes *Four Freedoms*
	Studio burns down
1951	Paints *Saying Grace*
1953	Moves to Stockbridge, Massachusetts
1959	Wife Mary dies
1961	Marries Molly Punderson
1963	Last cover for *The Saturday Evening Post* is published
1976	Last magazine cover appears on *American Artist*
1977	Receives Presidential Medal of Freedom
1978	November 8, dies at the age of eighty-four
1993	Norman Rockwell Museum opens in Stockbridge, Massachusetts
2013	The painting *Saying Grace* sells for $46 million

Timeline of the World

1895 — Abolitionist Frederick Douglass dies in Washington, DC

1903 — The Wright Brothers fly their airplane, the *Wright Flyer*, at Kitty Hawk, North Carolina

1914 — World War I begins

1918 — World War I ends

1920 — The Nineteenth Amendment is ratified, giving US women the right to vote

1929 — The US stock market crashes, setting off the Great Depression

1930 — Construction begins on the Empire State Building in New York City

1937 — Disney's *Snow White and the Seven Dwarfs* is released

1939 — World War II begins

1945 — World War II ends

1947 — Mahatma Gandhi begins a march for peace in India

1957 — Dr. Seuss's *The Cat in the Hat* is published

1962 — American pop artist Andy Warhol paints *Campbell's Soup Cans*

1963 — President John F. Kennedy assassinated in Dallas, Texas

1975 — End of the Vietnam War

2012 — NASA's Curiosity rover lands on Mars

Bibliography

*Books for young readers

*Cohen, Joel H. *Norman Rockwell: America's Best-Loved Illustrator.* Danbury, CT: Franklin Watts, 1997.

*Gherman, Beverly. *Norman Rockwell: Storyteller With a Brush.* New York: Atheneum, 2000.

Kamp, David. "Norman Rockwell's American Dream." *Vanity Fair*, October 7, 2009, www.vanityfair.com/culture/2009/11/norman-rockwell-200911.

Keillor, Garrison. "Norman Rockwell, the Storyteller: 'American Mirror: The Life and Art of Norman Rockwell,' by Deborah Solomon." *The New York Times*, December 19, 2013, www.nytimes.com/2013/12/22/books/review/american-mirror-the-life-and-art-of-norman-rockwell-by-deborah-solomon.html.

Marling, Karal Ann. *Norman Rockwell: 1894–1978: America's Most Beloved Painter.* Cologne, Germany: Taschen, 2005.

Rockwell, Norman. *My Adventures as an Illustrator.* New York: Abrams, 1988.

Solomon, Deborah. *American Mirror: The Life and Art of Norman Rockwell.* New York: Picador, 2013.

Stewart, James B. "Norman Rockwell's Art, Once Sniffed At, Is Becoming Prized." *The New York Times,* May 23, 2014, www.nytimes.com/2014/05/24/business/norman-rockwell-captures-the-art-markets-eye.html.

*Taylor, Charlotte. *Famous Artists: Get to Know Norman Rockwell.* New York: Enslow Publishing, 2016.

*Venezia, Mike. *Norman Rockwell.* Danbury, CT: Children's Press, 2000.

Website

Norman Rockwell: Biography

www.biography.com/people/norman-rockwell-37249